YOU HAVE WHAT IT TAKES!
You Can Do All Things Through Christ Who Strengthens You
Philippians 4:13

YOU HAVE
WHAT IT TAKES!

A 30-DAY DEVOTIONAL JOURNEY

BOB AND MICHELLE CAVINDER

Credits

You Have What It Takes! A 30-Day Devotional Journey
Written and Compiled by Bob and Michelle Cavinder
© 2025 Life by Design

Authors & Visionaries

Bob and Michelle Cavinder
Executive Directors, Life by Design
Speakers, Trainers, Facilitators, Life and Leadership Coaches
www.lifebydesign.net

This devotional is born out of years of mentoring, coaching, and training individuals who long to live with purpose and passion. It reflects Bob and Michelle's deep commitment to helping people discover that they truly do have what it takes — because God put it in them.

Table of Contents

Section 4: Victory & Vision

Introduction

We All Have a Mountain to Climb

At some point in life, we all stand at the foot of a mountain—an overwhelming task, a painful past, a new beginning, a bold dream, or a personal battle that looms large before us. We look up and wonder, do I really have what it takes? That question echoes in our hearts more than we often admit. It's the silent doubt beneath our daily efforts. It's the fear that keeps us playing small. And it's the lie that keeps us from fully becoming who God created us to be.

But here's the truth: You do have what it takes. Not because of who you are, but because of who God is within you.

This devotional isn't just another collection of inspirational readings—it's a journey of transformation. It's an invitation to lean into the truth of who you are in Christ and to climb your mountain—not in your own strength, but in the strength of the One who created you, called you, and is walking beside you every step of the way.

Every mountain in your life—whether it's climbing out of shame, pressing forward through grief, building a new dream, or simply surviving a season of waiting—is not meant to break you. It's meant to build you, shape you, and reveal the God-given courage, calling, and capacity within you.

Over the next 30 days, you will discover how:

- Your identity in Christ is stronger than your insecurities.
- God's grace is bigger than your past mistakes.
- His purpose for you is greater than your fear.
- And His power is more than enough for the climb ahead.

Each devotional includes:

- A foundational Scripture.
- A meaningful quote to reflect.
- A full-length devotional thought with biblical insight.
- A practical illustration from everyday life.
- Bold action points to move forward.
- Deep, reflective questions for journaling.
- A heartfelt prayer to anchor the day.

Our hope and prayer is that by the end of this journey, you will stop second-guessing yourself, stop disqualifying yourself, and start walking with holy confidence. You are not here by accident. You are here on assignment. God created you with purpose, for purpose, and He has equipped you with everything you need for live a godly life.

So yes, you may still be climbing. The mountain may still be steep. But you are no longer climbing alone, and you are no longer climbing without truth.

This is your reminder. This is your moment. You have what it takes. Now, let's climb together!

- Bob and Michelle Cavinder

Section Overview & Devotional Goals

Section 1: Identity & Strength

Focus: Knowing who you are in Christ and the strength Christ provides.

Goals for Section 1:

- Reclaim your identity in Christ.
- Find strength in God's presence, not your performance.
- Begin to believe you are capable of the climb.

Section 2: Calling & Courage

Focus: Discovering your unique purpose and taking brave steps of faith.

Goals for Section 2:

- Clarify your calling and spiritual direction.
- Take courageous steps toward your God-given goals.
- Trust God's timing, even when it's not your own.

Section 3: Purpose & Provision

Focus: Trusting God's plan, grace, and resources as you live out your purpose.

Goals for Section 3:

- Deepen your trust in God's provision and grace.
- Walk in obedience even when the path is uncertain.
- Renew your strength and focus on your journey.

Section 4: Victory & Vision

Focus: Living confidently in who you are and what you are called to do.

Goals for Section 4:

- Celebrate your growth and God's victory in your life.
- Live from a place of faith, not fear.
- Step into your next chapter with courage, vision, and purpose.

Section 1: Identity & Strength

Day 1

You Are Not Alone on the Mountain

Scripture: Deuteronomy 31:6

"Be strong and courageous. Do not be afraid or terrified because of them, for the LORD your God goes with you; he will never leave you nor forsake you."

Quote:

"Every mountain has a message — listen for God's voice in the wind." — Bob Cavinder

Devotional Thought:

Life's mountains can feel overwhelming. Whether it's a difficult relationship, a health challenge, or a career obstacle, it's easy to feel isolated and underprepared. But God's promise in Deuteronomy reminds us we are never alone. His presence surrounds us, strengthens us, and equips us for every climb. Your strength is not just your own—it is God's power working through you. The key to conquering your mountain is trusting that He is with you, and that you already have what it takes because His Spirit lives in you.

Illustration:

Imagine a young mountain climber standing at the base of a towering peak. Alone, the mountain looks impossible to scale. But she remembers that her guide, a seasoned climber, is beside her, holding the ropes and pointing the way. With each step, she feels more confident—not because the mountain has become smaller, but because her guide's presence makes her strong. God is that guide for you—steadfast, skilled, and always by your side.

Action Points:

Write down the mountain or challenge you are currently facing.

Reflect on past moments when God's presence encouraged or strengthened you.

Take one small step today, trusting God to guide you.

Reflective Questions:

- What mountain are you facing right now?
- How have you experienced God's presence in your struggles?
- What fears can you hand over to God today?

Prayer:

Heavenly Father,

Thank You for Your faithful presence that never leaves me. When I look at the mountains before me, it's easy to feel overwhelmed and alone, but You remind me that You are my strength and guide. Help me to walk each step with courage and trust, knowing that with You, I have what it takes. Teach me to lean on Your power and not my own and fill me with peace and confidence today. Walk with me in every challenge and help me to keep my eyes fixed on You. In Jesus' name, Amen

Day 2

Strength in Your Weakness

Scripture: 2 Corinthians 12:9

"My grace is sufficient for you, for my power is made perfect in weakness."

Quote:

"Our greatest weakness lies in giving up. The most certain way to succeed is always to try just one more time." — Thomas Edison

Devotional Thought:

It's natural to want to be strong all the time, but God's Word teaches us that His power shines brightest when we are weak. Your weaknesses are not obstacles but opportunities for God's grace and strength to be revealed. When you feel inadequate or incapable, it's a chance to depend more deeply on God. Rather than hiding your weaknesses, invite God into them. His strength will cover you, and you will find that you do, in fact, have what it takes through Him.

Illustration:

Consider a fragile seed planted in the soil. Alone, it looks weak and powerless, but under the surface, it's growing strong roots that will soon push through the earth into the sunlight. Like that seed, your weaknesses may seem small and insignificant, but God is working within you to develop strength that can overcome any mountain.

Action Points:

- Identify one weakness or fear you feel today.
- Ask God to show you how He can work through it.
- Share your struggle with a trusted friend or mentor for encouragement.

Reflective Questions:

- What weaknesses have you been trying to hide or overcome on your own?
- How might God want to use your weakness for His glory?
- Who can you invite to support you on your climb?

Prayer:

Lord God,

Thank You that Your grace is enough for me, even when I feel weak. Help me to stop striving in my own strength and to lean fully on Your power. Teach me to see my weaknesses as places where You can show up and do amazing things. Give me courage to be honest about my struggles and to trust that You are making me stronger every day. Fill me with Your peace as I climb the mountains ahead. In Jesus' name, Amen.

Day 3

One Step at a Time

> **Scripture: Psalm 37:23**
>
> "The LORD makes firm the steps of the one who delights in him."
>
> **Quote:**
>
> "The journey of a thousand miles begins with one step." — Lao Tzu

Devotional Thought:

Mountains don't get climbed in one giant leap—they are conquered step by step. Sometimes, it's easy to get discouraged by how far you still have to go or how heavy the burden feels. But God promises to steady your steps as you delight in Him. Focus on each small step of obedience, faith, or action today. Celebrate progress, not perfection. With God's guidance, each step builds strength, resilience, and momentum toward the summit.

Illustration:

Picture a toddler learning to walk. The first few steps are shaky, slow, and uncertain. But each time they try, their balance improves, their confidence grows, and eventually, running and climbing become possible. Life's mountains are no different. Your first steps may feel unsteady, but God's steady hand is guiding you onward.

Action Points:

- Break your big goal into small, manageable steps.
- Commit to taking one small action today toward your goal.
- Keep a journal to track progress and celebrate small victories.

Reflective Questions:

- What small step can you take today toward overcoming your challenge?
- How can you remind yourself daily that progress, not speed, is important?
- What distractions or fears keep you from moving forward?

Prayer:

Gracious Father,

Thank You for guiding each step I take. When I feel overwhelmed by the mountain before me, help me to focus on the step right in front of me. Give me patience and perseverance to keep moving forward, trusting that You are making my path straight. Remind me that with each step, I am stronger and closer to the victory You have promised. Strengthen my faith and keep my eyes fixed on You. In Jesus' name, Amen.

Day 4

Trusting God's Timing

Scripture: Ecclesiastes 3:1

"There is a time for everything, and a season for every activity under the heavens."

Quote:

"Patience is not simply the ability to wait – it's how we behave while we're waiting." — Joyce Meyer

Devotional Thought:

Mountains are climbed in seasons. Sometimes we want to rush ahead, to see immediate results or answers, but God's timing is perfect—even when it feels slow or confusing. Trusting God means surrendering your agenda and resting in His perfect plan. Each delay or detour is part of your preparation and growth. When you surrender your timeline, you will find peace and strength to keep climbing, knowing that God is making your path smooth at the right time.

Illustration:

Think of a farmer planting seeds. They must wait patiently for rain, sunshine, and the right season to see a harvest. They cannot rush the process, but they trust the natural order. Like the farmer, trusting God's timing means waiting faithfully and preparing yourself for the harvest that will come.

Action Points:

- Reflect on a time when God's timing proved perfect in your life.

- Write down areas where you struggle to wait on God.

- Choose to trust God's timing today through prayer and obedience.

Reflective Questions:

- Are you trying to control something that God wants to handle in His time?

- How can waiting well be an act of faith?

- What does trusting God's timing look like in your current situation?

Prayer:

Father,

Help me to trust Your perfect timing in every area of my life. When I feel impatient or anxious, remind me that You are working all things for my good. Teach me to wait well, to prepare my heart and mind, and to keep climbing even when I can't see the summit yet. Fill me with peace and confidence in Your plan. I surrender my timeline into Your hands. In Jesus' name, Amen.

Day 5

God's Strength is Your Anchor

Scripture: Isaiah 40:31

"But those who hope in the LORD will renew their strength. They will soar on wings like eagles; they will run and not grow weary, they will walk and not be faint."

Quote:

"Faith is taking the first step even when you don't see the whole staircase." — Martin Luther King Jr.

Devotional Thought:

Climbing mountains can leave you tired, discouraged, and ready to give up. But God offers a wellspring of strength when you put your hope and trust in Him. This strength isn't temporary or superficial—it's a deep renewal that lifts you up when you feel weak. You don't have to rely on your own energy. When your strength runs low, God's power fills you. Anchor your hope in Him, and you will find the endurance to keep climbing, even when the path is hard.

Illustration:

Imagine an eagle soaring high above the mountain, riding powerful winds with ease. It doesn't flap its wings constantly but trusts the currents to carry it forward. God's strength is like that wind—unseen but powerful—lifting you above your struggles and carrying you to the summit.

Action Points:

- Identify areas where you feel weary or weak.

- Ask God to renew your strength daily.

- Memorize Isaiah 40:31 to remind yourself of God's power.

Reflective Questions:

- Where do you need God's strength most right now?

- How can you place your hope in God instead of your own efforts?

- What practical habits help you stay spiritually strong?

Prayer:

Lord God,

Thank You that Your strength is made perfect when I am weak. I place my hope in You and ask for renewed energy and courage for this climb. Help me to rely on Your power, not my own, and to soar above the challenges that weigh me down. Fill me with endurance and faith to keep moving forward. Be my anchor and my guide every step of the way. In Jesus' name, Amen.

Day 6

Courage to Face the Unknown

Scripture: Joshua 1:9

"Have I not commanded you? Be strong and courageous. Do not be afraid; do not be discouraged, for the LORD your God will be with you wherever you go."

Quote:

"Courage doesn't mean you don't get afraid. Courage means you don't let fear stop you." — Bethany Hamilton

Devotional Thought:

Facing the unknown can be terrifying. Mountains often appear intimidating because we can't see what's beyond the next ridge. But God commands courage, not because the path will be easy, but because He is with you every step. Courage is not the absence of fear—it's moving forward in faith despite fear. When you lean on God, you discover that you have what it takes to face uncertainty and press on with confidence.

Illustration:

Think of a hiker at night, unable to see the trail clearly. The darkness is scary, but the flashlight in their hand lights the way step by step. God is your light in the unknown, guiding and strengthening you to keep climbing even when the path is unclear.

Action Points:

- Identify an area where fear is holding you back.

- Pray for God's courage to face that fear today.

- Take a small step forward despite your fear.

Reflective Questions:

- What fears do you need to surrender to God today?

- How can courage grow when you rely on God's presence?

- Who encourages you to be courageous in your life?

Prayer:

Father God,

Thank You that You are always with me—even in the unknown. When fear tries to paralyze me, give me courage to move forward. Help me to trust Your presence more than my feelings and to take steps of faith, even when I don't see the whole path. Remind me that with You, I have everything I need to overcome fear. In Jesus' name, Amen.

Day 7

Focus on the Summit, Not the Struggle

Scripture: Philippians 3:14

"I press on toward the goal to win the prize for which God has called me heavenward in Christ Jesus."

Quote:

"When faced with a mountain, I WILL NOT QUIT! I will keep on striving until I climb over, find a pass through, tunnel underneath, or simply stay and turn the mountain into a gold mine with God's help!" — Dr. Robert H. Schuller

Devotional Thought:

It's easy to get discouraged by the hard parts of the climb—the fatigue, the setbacks, the obstacles. But God invites us to fix our eyes on the goal He has set before us. When your vision is clear, the struggle loses its power to defeat you. The mountain becomes a pathway, and every challenge is a step closer to the prize God has promised. Your future with God is bright and victorious, so keep pressing on with faith and hope.

Illustration:

Imagine you are a runner in a race. The miles are long and the course tough, but keep your gaze on the finish line, hearing the cheers and feeling the joy ahead. When the climb feels overwhelming, remember that your goal is worth every step.

Action Points:

- Visualize your "summit" or goal in detail.
- Write down the promises of God that motivate you.
- When discouraged, remind yourself of your goal and God's faithfulness.

Reflective Questions:

- What is the summit you are aiming for?
- How can focusing on God's promises help you persevere?
- What distractions or discouragements steal your focus?

Prayer:

Lord Jesus,

Help me to keep my eyes on You and the prize You have set before me. When I'm tempted to focus on my struggles, remind me of Your promises and the victory ahead. Strengthen my heart to press on with hope and joy, knowing that You are guiding me every step of the way. Let my faith grow stronger each day as I climb the mountains You have called me to conquer. In Your name, Amen.

Section 2: Calling & Courage

Day 8

Prepared for Every Step

Scripture: Ephesians 6:11

"Put on the full armor of God, so that you can take your stand against the devil's schemes."

Quote:

"Preparation is the key to success." — Alexander Graham Bell

Devotional Thought:

Climbing any mountain requires preparation. Spiritually, God equips us with His armor—truth, righteousness, peace, faith, salvation, and the Word of God—to stand firm against challenges and discouragement. Preparation is more than just physical readiness; it's about being spiritually fortified for every battle on the climb. When you put on God's armor daily, you gain confidence to face whatever comes your way because you have what it takes from heaven itself.

Illustration:

A soldier never goes into battle unprepared. They train, put on armor, and ready their weapons. Similarly, your spiritual preparation is your armor for the climb. The mountain may be steep, but you are armored and ready through God's power.

Action Points:

- Commit to daily prayer and Bible reading as spiritual preparation.

- Identify areas in your life where you need God's armor more fully.

- Practice putting on God's armor each morning with intention.

Reflective Questions:

- What spiritual tools do you need to rely on more?

- How can daily preparation change your perspective on challenges?

- Are there habits you need to build to stay spiritually strong?

Prayer:

Lord,

Thank You for equipping me with Your armor to stand strong. Help me to put on Your protection daily and to be vigilant against anything that would discourage or distract me. Prepare my heart and mind to face every challenge with Your strength and wisdom. Keep me alert and ready as I climb the mountains before me. In Jesus' name, Amen.

Day 9

Rest for the Weary

Scripture: Matthew 11:28

"Come to me, all you who are weary and burdened, and I will give you rest."

Quote:

"Sometimes the most productive thing you can do is relax." — Mark Black

Devotional Thought:

Climbing a mountain is exhausting—both physically and emotionally. God knows this and invites you to find rest in Him. Rest doesn't mean giving up; it means recharging, renewing, and trusting God to carry you when you are weak. Taking time to rest is a vital part of the climb. It refreshes your soul, restores your strength, and prepares you to face the next challenge with renewed vigor.

Illustration:

Picture a hiker pausing on a ledge, breathing deeply, drinking water, and soaking in the beauty around them. That rest allows them to continue the journey stronger. God offers that same rest for your soul.

Action Points:

- Schedule intentional rest moments today to refresh your mind and spirit.

- Practice a calming prayer or meditation to experience God's peace.

- Identify signs of weariness and take action before burnout.

Reflective Questions:

- When was the last time you truly rested?

- How can rest be part of your spiritual journey?

- What habits drain your energy and need adjustment?

Prayer:

Dear Jesus,

Thank You for inviting me to come to You when I am weary. Help me to accept Your rest and allow You to renew my strength. Teach me to pause and listen to Your voice in the midst of busyness and struggle. Restore my soul and prepare me to keep climbing with joy and hope. In Your name, Amen.

Day 10

Keep Your Faith Alive

Scripture: Hebrews 11:1

"Now faith is confidence in what we hope for and assurance about what we do not see."

Quote:

"Mountains don't move because of strength, but because of faith." — Unknown

Devotional Thought:

Faith is the fuel that keeps you moving when the mountain seems insurmountable. It's believing in what you cannot yet see—God's promises, your purpose, and your victory. Keeping your faith alive means choosing to trust God every day, even when the evidence feels thin. Faith is a muscle that grows stronger with use. The more you rely on God and trust His Word, the more empowered you become to climb higher and overcome challenges.

Illustration:

Imagine a camper lighting a lantern on a dark night. The light doesn't erase the darkness, but it provides enough illumination to see the next step. Faith is that light on your path—guiding you through uncertainty toward the dawn of a new day.

Action Points:

- Read stories of faith in the Bible to inspire your trust in God.
- Write down promises from Scripture that encourage you.
- Practice speaking words of faith aloud when doubts arise.

Reflective Questions:

- How has faith helped you overcome past challenges?
- What doubts do you need to surrender to God today?
- How can you nurture your faith daily?

Prayer:

Faithful God,

Thank You for the gift of faith that sustains me through every challenge. Help me to keep my faith alive even when the climb feels difficult and the outcome uncertain. Strengthen my confidence in Your promises and teach me to trust You more each day. Let my faith be a light that guides me toward Your peace and victory. In Jesus' name, Amen.

Day 11

Overcoming Doubt

Scripture: Mark 9:23

"If you can? said Jesus. Everything is possible for one who believes."

Quote:

"Doubt kills more dreams than failure ever will." — Suzy Kassem

Devotional Thought:

Doubt is a common companion on every mountain climb. It whispers, "You are not strong enough," or "This is too hard." But Jesus reminds us that faith opens the door to the impossible. Doubt tries to paralyze your progress, but belief activates God's power in your life. When doubt creeps in, fight it with the truth of God's promises and the reality of His past faithfulness. You have what it takes—because God is bigger than your doubts.

Illustration:

Picture a tightrope walker suspended high above the ground. If they focus on the height and the risk, fear overwhelms them. But if they focus on the sturdy rope and their skill, they can cross with confidence. Doubt is like looking down—the way forward is trusting the rope and your ability.

Action Points:

- Identify doubts that are holding you back.

- Replace each doubt with a Bible verse or positive truth.

- Pray for increased faith and courage to believe God's promises.

Reflective Questions:

- What doubts have you been struggling with recently?

- How does God's Word speak into those doubts?

- What steps can you take to choose faith over fear?

Prayer:

Lord Jesus,

Thank You for reminding me that with faith, all things are possible. When doubt threatens to stop me, help me to remember Your power and promises. Strengthen my belief and give me courage to keep climbing, knowing You are with me. Help me to fix my eyes on You and not on my fears. In Your name, Amen.

Day 12

God Works All Things for Good

Scripture: Romans 8:28

"And we know that in all things God works for the good of those who love him, who have been called according to his purpose."

Quote:

"Sometimes the bad things that happen in our lives put us directly on the path to the best things that will ever happen to us." — Unknown

Devotional Thought:

Mountains often come with pain, setbacks, and disappointment. But God is always working behind the scenes, turning difficulties into blessings. Even when you don't see it, He is weaving your story together for good. This truth gives hope that no mountain is wasted and no struggle is meaningless. When you trust God's purpose, you realize that you truly have what it takes—because God uses everything in your life to prepare you for His plan.

Illustration:

Think of a tapestry that looks like a tangled mess on the back but reveals a beautiful design on the front. God is the master weaver, turning every trial into part of a magnificent picture.

Action Points:

- Reflect on past struggles that later brought growth or blessing.

- Write down ways God has worked for your good.

- Choose to trust God's plan today, even when you don't understand.

Reflective Questions:

- What struggles are you facing that feel overwhelming?

- How can trusting God's plan bring peace in the middle of hardship?

- In what ways has God already shown His goodness in your life?

Prayer:

Gracious God,

Thank You that You work all things together for my good. Help me to trust Your purpose even when I can't see the full picture. Teach me to surrender my pain and struggles to You and to believe that You are making something beautiful in my life. Give me patience and hope as I continue this climb, knowing You are faithful. In Jesus' name, Amen.

Day 13

Strength Through Christ

Scripture: Philippians 4:13

"I can do all things through Christ who strengthens me."

Quote:

"You were given this life because you are strong enough to live it." — Unknown

Devotional Thought:

Your strength is not based on your own ability but on Christ's power working within you. Whatever mountain you face, God's strength is available to you. It's a supernatural strength that carries you when you are weak, motivates you when you are tired, and empowers you when you feel like giving up. Remember, you are stronger than you think—not because of who you are, but because of who is in you.

Illustration:

Imagine a battery-powered device that runs smoothly as long as it's connected to its power source. When disconnected, it quickly dies. Your life is like that device—connected to Christ, you have endless strength to keep going.

Action Points:

- Memorize Philippians 4:13 and recite it daily.

- Ask God to fill you with His strength when you feel weak.

- Reflect on moments when God's strength helped you overcome.

Reflective Questions:

- When have you felt God's strength most clearly in your life?

- What areas do you need to rely on Christ's strength more?

- How can remembering this truth change your daily perspective?

Prayer:

Lord Jesus,

Thank You that I can do all things through You who gives me strength. When I feel weak or overwhelmed, remind me to lean on Your power. Fill me with Your strength each day so I can face every mountain with confidence. Help me to live boldly, knowing that You are the source of my courage and endurance. In Your name, Amen.

Day 14

You Are Called to Make a Difference

Scripture: Matthew 5:14

"You are the light of the world. A town built on a hill cannot be hidden."

Quote:

"What you do makes a difference, and you have to decide what kind of difference you want to make." — Jane Goodall

Devotional Thought:

You have been created for purpose. Your life matters and your actions impact others. The mountains you climb aren't just for you—they are preparation for the difference God wants you to make in the world. When you live with intention and faith, your light shines bright, encouraging others and bringing hope. You have what it takes because God's purpose for your life is greater than any challenge you face.

Illustration:

Think of a lighthouse standing tall on a rocky shore. It may face storms and waves, but its light guides sailors safely through the darkness. Like that lighthouse, you are called to shine even when the climb is hard.

Action Points:

- Identify ways your story can inspire or help others.

- Look for opportunities to serve or encourage someone today.

- Pray for clarity about your unique purpose and impact.

Reflective Questions:

- How has your journey prepared you to make a difference?

- What gifts or passions can you use to serve others?

- How can you shine your light even in difficult times?

Prayer:

God of Purpose,

Thank You for calling me to be a light in this world. Help me to understand the impact I can have and to live with intention each day. Strengthen me to climb the mountains You have set before me so I can be an encouragement and blessing to others. Use my life to bring hope and light where there is darkness. In Jesus' name, Amen.

Section 3: Purpose & Provision

Day 15

Victory is Within Your Reach

Scripture: 1 Corinthians 15:57

"But thanks be to God! He gives us the victory through our Lord Jesus Christ."

Quote:

"Victory is always possible for the person who refuses to stop fighting." — Napoleon Hill

Devotional Thought:

The summit is closer than you think. Victory is not just a distant dream—it's a reality promised by God through Jesus Christ. No matter how steep or difficult the climb, God equips you to reach the top. Keep your heart focused on His strength and promises. Victory is not earned by your strength alone, but by the power of Christ living in you. With God, you truly have what it takes to overcome and triumph.

Illustration:

Imagine a marathon runner in the final stretch, feeling exhausted but pushing forward with every ounce of strength. The finish line is just ahead, and the crowd cheers. You are that runner, and God is cheering you on toward victory.

Action Points:

- Celebrate small victories in your journey so far.

- Remind yourself daily of God's promise of victory.

- Share your progress with someone who can encourage you.

Reflective Questions:

- What victories have you already experienced in your climb?

- How can focusing on God's promise keep you motivated?

- What keeps you going when the journey feels hard?

Prayer:

Almighty God,

Thank You for the victory You have won for me through Jesus Christ. Help me to keep pressing forward, confident that the summit is within reach. When I feel weary or discouraged, remind me of Your power at work in me. Fill me with hope and courage to keep climbing, knowing that with You, victory is assured. In Jesus' name, Amen.

Day 16

Trusting God's Provision

Scripture: Philippians 4:19

"And my God will meet all your needs according to the riches of his glory in Christ Jesus."

Quote:

"Where God guides, He provides." — Unknown

Devotional Thought:

One of the greatest struggles on the climb is wondering whether you will have what you need to keep going—strength, resources, support, direction. But God promises to supply every need, not according to your limited ability, but according to His infinite riches. His provision may not always come the way you expect, but it always comes right on time. When you trust in His provision, you move forward in peace, knowing that your Father is watching every step and equipping you for the journey.

Illustration:

Imagine a traveler in the desert running low on water. Just as their canteen runs dry, they find an oasis with fresh springs. That's what God's provision looks like—exactly what you need, exactly when you need it. He sees your need before you even speak it.

Action Points:

- List current needs you are praying for—physical, emotional, or spiritual.

- Reflect on past times God provided unexpectedly.

- Take one step of faith today that shows your trust in His provision.

Reflective Questions:

- What area of your life feels most uncertain right now?

- Are you looking to God or to your own strength for provision?

- How has God proven Himself faithful in the past?

Prayer:

Faithful Father,

Thank You for the promise that You will supply all of my needs. Forgive me when I worry or try to solve everything on my own. Today, I release every fear, need, and concern into Your hands. Provide for me as only You can. Help me to trust that You know what's best and that You will not let me go without. Teach me to depend on You with all my heart. In Jesus' name, Amen.

Day 17

Embracing God's Grace

Scripture: 2 Corinthians 12:9

"But he said to me, My grace is sufficient for you, for my power is made perfect in weakness."

Quote:

"Grace means that all of your mistakes now serve a purpose instead of serving shame." — Brené Brown

Devotional Thought:

We all stumble. We all fall short. But God's grace is the safety net that catches us and lifts us back up. Grace isn't earned—it's freely given. It reminds you that no mistake disqualifies you from the mountain God has called you to climb. His grace covers your past and strengthens your present. When you embrace grace, you stop striving to prove your worth and start walking in the freedom of being fully loved. That's what gives you the courage to keep climbing.

Illustration:

Picture a child learning to ride a bike. When they fall, a loving parent doesn't scold—they help them back up, brush off the dirt, and encourage them to try again. That's how God's grace works. It's patient, present, and powerful.

Action Points:

- Reflect on areas where you've been hard on yourself.

- Ask God to show you how He sees you—loved, forgiven, and chosen.

- Show grace to someone else today as God has shown to you.

Reflective Questions:

- Where do you need to receive God's grace more fully?

- How would your perspective shift if you lived like grace is enough?

- Who in your life needs to experience grace from you?

Prayer:

God of Mercy,

Thank You for Your grace that covers me every day. I've made mistakes, but You never stop loving me. Teach me to walk in the freedom and power of Your grace. Help me to stop trying to earn Your love and instead rest in what You've already given. Let grace lead me as I climb higher. In Jesus' name, Amen.

Day 18

Walking in Obedience

Scripture: John 14:15

"If you love me, keep my commands."

Quote:

"Obedience is the key that unlocks God's blessings." — Charles Stanley

Devotional Thought:

Every step of your climb involves a choice: will you follow your own way or God's way? Obedience is not about perfection—it's about trust. It's saying, "God, even when I don't understand, I'll follow You." When you obey God's leading, even in the small things, He opens doors and makes the mountain climb possible. Obedience builds faith, shapes character, and strengthens your steps.

Illustration:

Think of a GPS on a road trip. When you follow the directions, you arrive safely—even when you don't understand every turn. But ignoring the guidance leads to wrong paths and delays. Obedience is your spiritual GPS, guiding you to God's best.

Action Points:

- Ask God if there's an area where He's calling you to obey more fully.

- Take one obedient step, even if it feels small or uncomfortable.

- Write a prayer of surrender to God's will.

Reflective Questions:

- What is God asking you to do that you've been resisting?

- How have you seen obedience lead to blessings in your life?

- How can you build a heart that delights in following God?

Prayer:

Lord,

Help me to follow You with a willing heart. Even when obedience feels hard, remind me that Your way is always best. Give me strength to take steps of faith and trust in Your plan. I surrender my own understanding and desires to walk in the path You've laid before me. In Jesus' name, Amen.

Day 19

Renewed Strength

Scripture: Isaiah 40:29

"He gives strength to the weary and increases the power of the weak."

Quote:

"Sometimes, when you are in a dark place, you think you've been buried, but actually you've been planted." — Christine Caine

Devotional Thought:

Exhaustion is part of the climb. There are days when your strength feels depleted, when your passion wanes, and your heart is heavy. But God promises to renew your strength. He's not asking you to climb on empty—He's offering divine power for every step. When you pause, pray, and wait on Him, He fills your soul with fresh endurance. His renewal is like a fresh wind beneath your wings, lifting you higher.

Illustration:

Think of a phone battery drained from overuse. You plug it in, and in time, it's restored to full power. Likewise, time in God's presence is the recharge your spirit needs. You don't have to do this alone or in your own energy.

Action Points:

- Set aside quiet time today just to rest in God's presence.
- Journal about what's been draining your strength lately.
- Choose one healthy practice to refresh your body and spirit.

Reflective Questions:

- Where are you feeling weary in your life?
- How can you let God restore your strength today?
- What rhythms of rest and renewal can you build into your life?

Prayer:

Father,

I come to You weary and worn. I need Your strength today more than ever. Breathe new life into my soul and renew my energy for the journey ahead. Help me to slow down, listen, and rest in You. Teach me to walk in rhythms of grace instead of striving in my own effort. I receive Your promise of renewed strength with gratitude. In Jesus' name, Amen.

Day 20

Courage to Step Forward

Scripture: Psalm 56:3

"When I am afraid, I put my trust in you."

Quote:

"Fear is a reaction. Courage is a decision." — Winston Churchill

Devotional Thought:

There comes a moment in every journey when you must decide to take the next step—even when fear lingers. Courage isn't about the absence of fear; it's choosing faith over fear. Fear freezes us. Faith moves us forward. When you place your trust in God, courage rises. The mountain may not move, but your confidence does. You have what it takes to keep climbing because the One who leads you is fearless and faithful.

Illustration:

Think of a child standing at the edge of a swimming pool, scared to jump. Their parent is in the water, arms outstretched. All it takes is trust. That leap of faith is where courage is born—and joy follows.

Action Points:

- Identify something you've been afraid to step into.
- Write down what trusting God in that area looks like.
- Take one small action today that reflects courage.

Reflective Questions:

- What step have you been hesitating to take?
- How can trusting God help you move forward with courage?
- What encouragement from Scripture strengthens your resolve?

Prayer:

Lord of All,

Give me courage today to take the next step forward. I confess that fear sometimes holds me back, but I choose to place my trust in You. Remind me that You go before me and that I am never alone. Strengthen my heart and lead me in boldness. I know You are faithful, and I want to follow You with confidence. In Jesus' name, Amen.

:

Day 21

Joy in the Journey

Scripture: Nehemiah 8:10

"The joy of the LORD is your strength."

Quote:

"Joy is not in things; it is in us." — Richard Wagner

Devotional Thought:

Climbing a mountain is not just about reaching the summit—it's about how you grow, what you learn, and who you become along the way. While the journey is often difficult, joy can be found in the process. Joy is not based on circumstances; it comes from God's presence within you. His joy gives you strength, endurance, and resilience. Even when the path is steep, His joy reminds you that life with Him is worth every step.

Illustration:

Think of a hiker who stops midway through the climb, not because they've reached the top, but to breathe in the beauty around them. They smile—not because the hike is easy, but because the journey itself is meaningful. That's what joy in the journey looks like.

Action Points:

- Find one moment today to pause and thank God for where you are.
- Choose gratitude in a difficult moment.
- Share something joyful with someone else today.

Reflective Questions:

- Where have you seen God's joy carry you through a hard season?
- How can you choose joy today regardless of your circumstances?
- What can you celebrate right now, even before the summit?

Prayer:

Lord of Joy,

Thank You for being the source of joy in my life. Teach me to embrace joy, even when the journey is hard. Let Your joy strengthen me and shine through me. Open my eyes to see the blessings around me and help me to walk in gratitude and peace. Remind me that the journey is just as important as the destination. In Jesus' name, Amen.

Section 4: Victory & Vision

Day 22

Your Story Has Purpose

Scripture: Revelation 12:11

"They triumphed over him by the blood of the Lamb and by the word of their testimony."

Quote:

"Your story is the key that can unlock someone else's prison." — Unknown

Devotional Thought:

Every step, every scar, every setback on your mountain has shaped your story—and your story has purpose. God uses what you've walked through not just for your growth, but to encourage and empower others. When you share your testimony, you remind others they're not alone. Your story, empowered by God's grace, is a weapon against discouragement and doubt. You have what it takes not just to overcome—but to help others do the same.

Illustration:

Imagine a guide leading others up a mountain they've already climbed. Their experience gives others hope. Your story is that guide—lighting the way for someone behind you.

Action Points:

- Reflect on a powerful part of your story.

- Share your testimony with someone who may need encouragement.

- Thank God for using your past to build someone else's future.

Reflective Questions:

- What part of your story has God redeemed for a greater purpose?

- Who could benefit from hearing how God has worked in your life?

- How can your testimony bring hope to others?

Prayer:

God of Redemption,

Thank You for giving purpose to my story. Help me to see how You've used every mountain, every valley, and every lesson to shape me. Give me courage to share my journey and the wisdom to know when and how. Use my story to bring light to others and to glorify You. In Jesus' name, Amen.

Day 23

Equipped for the Calling

Scripture: Hebrews 13:21

"...equip you with everything good for doing his will, and may he work in us what is pleasing to him, through Jesus Christ..."

Quote:

"God doesn't call the qualified. He qualifies the called." — Unknown

Devotional Thought:

God will never ask you to climb a mountain without giving you what you need. He equips those He calls. Even when you feel underprepared, God has already placed within you the strength, skills, and spirit necessary for the climb. Trust His preparation. Every past experience, lesson, and even failure has shaped you for this moment. Step into your calling knowing that you are not lacking—you are equipped.

Illustration:

Picture an emergency responder. They don't know what each call will require, but their gear is packed, their training complete, and their trust strong. They are equipped, ready to respond. You, too, are equipped for the mission God has given you.

Action Points:

- List the tools, experiences, or lessons God has given you for your current challenge.

- Ask God to reveal any areas where He wants to grow you further.

- Step out in faith, trusting in the preparation He's done in you.

Reflective Questions:

- What has God used in your past to prepare you for today?

- Where are you underestimating what God has equipped you to do?

- What does obedience look like in your current calling?

Prayer:

Heavenly Father,

Thank You for equipping me with what I need to fulfill Your purpose for my life. Remind me that I don't climb in my own strength, but with Your power, wisdom, and provision. Strengthen my confidence in Your preparation. I am ready—not because I am perfect, but because You are faithful. In Jesus' name, Amen.

Day 24

Love Makes You Strong

Scripture: 1 Corinthians 16:14

"Do everything in love."

Quote:

"Love is the most powerful force in the world." — Martin Luther King Jr.

Devotional Thought (continued):

…Even when the mountain is steep and the path uncertain, love gives you the reason to keep going. God's love for you is unshakable—and when that love flows through you, it makes you a force for healing, strength, and purpose in the lives of others. When you love deeply, serve selflessly, and live generously, you reflect God's heart—and that reflection makes you strong.

Illustration:

Think of a parent carrying a child up a long hill. Their legs may ache, but their love pushes them forward with energy they didn't know they had. That's the power of love—it makes burdens bearable and sacrifices worthwhile.

Action Points:

- Look for one way today to show love that costs you something.

- Reflect on how God's love has sustained you during hard times.

- Speak words of love and encouragement to someone climbing their own mountain.

Reflective Questions:

- How has God's love made you stronger in your journey?

- Who in your life needs to be reminded of love's strength?

- What would it look like for you to "do everything in love" this Section?

Prayer:

Loving God,

Thank You that Your love is my anchor, my fuel, and my strength. Teach me to walk in that love every day—not just in words, but in action. Let my life reflect the power of love in the way I serve, lead, and climb. Fill my heart with compassion, and use me to be a source of strength to those around me. In Jesus' name, Amen.

Day 25

The Joy of the Lord Is Your Strength

Scripture: Nehemiah 8:10

"Do not grieve, for the joy of the LORD is your strength."

Quote:

"Joy is the serious business of Heaven." — C.S. Lewis

Devotional Thought:

There's a unique kind of strength that comes from joy—not fleeting happiness, but the deep-rooted joy found in the presence of God. This joy doesn't depend on circumstances or results; it flows from knowing who God is and who you are in Him. When the climb feels exhausting and setbacks come, joy lifts your spirit. It renews your energy, shifts your focus from pain to promise, and reminds you that even in the climb, you are victorious. Joy isn't just an emotion—it's your secret strength.

Illustration:

Imagine a group of hikers who, despite harsh weather and tough terrain, sing songs as they climb. Their joy doesn't change the mountain, but it changes them. Their attitude gives them strength to keep going. That's what joy from God looks like—it redefines how you face the climb.

Action Points:

- Choose one worship song or verse that brings you joy and meditate on it today.

- Find something to laugh about or be grateful for in the middle of your circumstances.

- Encourage someone else today with a joyful word or act.

Reflective Questions:

- Where does your joy come from on hard days?

- How can you make space for more joy in your daily walk with God?

- Who can you share joy with today?

Prayer:

God of Joy,

Thank You for the gift of joy that strengthens and sustains me. Even when the road is hard and long, Your joy fills my heart with hope and peace. Teach me to draw strength from the joy of being Yours. Help me to choose joy intentionally and to share it freely with others. Let my life reflect the goodness and gladness of walking with You. In Jesus' name, Amen.

Day 26

Courage for Your Future

Scripture: Jeremiah 29:11

"For I know the plans I have for you, declares the LORD, plans to prosper you and not to harm you, plans to give you hope and a future."

Quote:

"Courage is not the absence of fear, but rather the judgment that something else is more important than fear." — Ambrose Redmoon

Devotional Thought:

The future can be intimidating. We worry about the unknown, the "what ifs," and whether we'll be strong enough to face what's ahead. But God reassures us—He knows the plan. And not only that, His plan is good. When we anchor our hearts in this truth, courage rises. The same God who has brought you this far is already in your tomorrow. You can walk boldly forward, not because you have every answer, but because you walk with the One who does.

Illustration:

Picture a rock climber preparing to reach for the next ledge. They can't see what's above, but they trust the safety rope and their training. With a deep breath, they move forward. Like that climber, courage for the future comes when you trust the One securing your path.

Action Points:

- Write out any fears you have about the future and release them to God.

- Reflect on how God has been faithful in your past.

- Take a bold step toward something God is calling you to do.

Reflective Questions:

- What fears are keeping you from stepping forward?

- How does knowing God has a plan give you courage?

- What one step can you take today toward the future God has for you?

Prayer:

Father,

Thank You for having a plan for my life—one filled with hope and purpose. When fear rises, remind me of Your promises. Give me courage not just to dream about the future, but to walk into it with boldness. Help me to trust that You go before me, preparing the way and strengthening me every step of the journey. In Jesus' name, Amen.

Day 27

Faith Over Fear

Scripture: 2 Timothy 1:7

"For the Spirit God gave us does not make us timid, but gives us power, love and self-discipline."

Quote:

"Fear and faith have something in common—they both ask you to believe in something you cannot see." — Unknown

Devotional Thought:

Fear is real. But it doesn't have to be the loudest voice in your life. God has given you a different spirit—not one of fear, but one of power and love. Fear shrinks your world. Faith expands it. Every time you choose to believe God's promises over your insecurities, faith wins. Choosing faith isn't always easy, but it's always worth it. Let faith guide your steps as you climb, not fear.

Illustration:

Think of two seeds—one fear, one faith. The one you water is the one that grows. Water faith with prayer, Scripture, and trust, and it will bloom into courage. Starve fear by refusing to give it your attention.

Action Points:

- Identify one fear you've been feeding and make a choice to speak truth over it.

- Write out 2 Timothy 1:7 and place it where you will see it daily.

- Surround yourself with voices that build your faith, not your fear.

Reflective Questions:

- What fears have been dominating your thoughts lately?

- How can you intentionally feed your faith this Section?

- What does living in power and love look like for you right now?

Prayer:

Lord,

I thank You that You have not given me a spirit of fear. Replace my fear with faith today. Help me to choose belief over doubt and trust over anxiety. I ask You to strengthen me with power, fill me with love, and give me the discipline to walk confidently in Your promises. With You, fear has no hold on me. In Jesus' name, Amen.

Day 28

Endurance for the Race

Scripture: Hebrews 12:1

"...Let us run with perseverance the race marked out for us."

Quote:

"It does not matter how slowly you go, as long as you do not stop." — Confucius

Devotional Thought:

Endurance isn't flashy, but it's powerful. It's not about speed or perfection—it's about persistence. Life's mountain climbs require long-haul strength, the kind that keeps going even when emotions fade or progress feels slow. But endurance is built through consistency, faith, and grace. God isn't asking you to sprint—He's asking you to stay in the race. And He promises to supply everything you need to finish strong.

Illustration:

Think of a marathon runner pacing themselves through miles of challenge. Their secret isn't superhuman strength—it's unwavering consistency. They've trained. They've prepared. And with every step, they remember the goal. That's the endurance God calls you to walk in.

Action Points:

- Recommit to your journey today, no matter how slow your progress.

- Celebrate how far you've come, not just how far you have to go.

- Ask God to renew your endurance for the days ahead.

Reflective Questions:

- In what area of life are you tempted to give up?

- How has God carried you in moments of weariness before?

- What routines or habits can help you build spiritual endurance?

Prayer:

Heavenly Father,

Thank You for calling me to run my race with endurance. When I feel tired, remind me of the purpose and the prize. Help me not to compare my pace to others, but to stay faithful to the path You've marked out for me. Fill me with strength to keep going, trusting that You will help me finish well. In Jesus' name, Amen.

Day 29

Victory Is Yours

> **Scripture: Romans 8:37**
>
> "No, in all these things we are more than conquerors through him who loved us."
>
> **Quote:**
>
> "Victory belongs to the most persevering." — Napoleon Bonaparte

Devotional Thought:

You are not fighting for victory—you are fighting from it. Because of Jesus, victory is already yours. Whatever mountain you are facing—fear, failure, addiction, loss, doubt—Jesus has already overcome. That doesn't mean the climb won't be hard. But it does mean you are more than a conqueror. Don't just survive—stand tall in the identity and authority Christ has given you. Walk as someone who knows the ending: God wins, and you win with Him.

Illustration:

Imagine a championship team stepping onto the field already knowing the final score is in their favor. They still play, still fight—but they do so with confidence. That's your posture in Christ—victory has already been declared.

Action Points:

- Declare Romans 8:37 over your life today.

- Reflect on a past victory God has brought you through.

- Walk today with the mindset of a conqueror.

Reflective Questions:

- Where do you need to shift from defeat to victory mindset?

- How can walking in victory change the way you approach your challenges?

- What promises remind you of your identity in Christ?

Prayer:

Jesus,

Thank You that through You, I am more than a conqueror. I claim victory over every lie, obstacle, and fear trying to hold me back. Help me walk boldly in the truth of who I am in You. Let my life be marked by confidence, peace, and power—not because of my strength, but because of Yours. In Your name, Amen.

Day 30

You Have What It Takes

> **Scripture: 2 Peter 1:3**
>
> "His divine power has given us everything we need for a godly life through our knowledge of him who called us by his own glory and goodness."
>
> **Quote:**
>
> "Everything you need, you already have. You just have to believe it." — Unknown

Devotional Thought:

Here's the truth: you have what it takes—not because you are perfect, but because God is. His power, His presence, and His promises are already inside you. The mountain you are climbing may be steep, but you are not doing it alone. Every lesson, every trial, every triumph has brought you to this moment. The same God who called you is the One who equips you. Don't wait until you feel "ready." You are already equipped. You have what it takes—because God is with you and in you.

Illustration:

Think of a mountaineer who finally reaches the summit. As they look back at the trail, they realize every obstacle, every hardship was worth it. They didn't always feel strong—but they climbed anyway. That's you. Keep climbing. The view is worth it.

Action Points:

- Declare aloud: "Through Christ, I have what it takes."

- Encourage someone else who's on a climb of their own.

- Reflect on the transformation you've experienced in these 30 days.

Reflective Questions:

- What mountain have you climbed during this devotional journey?

- How has God reminded you that you have what it takes?

- How will you keep this truth alive in your daily life?

Prayer:

God of Glory,

Thank You for walking with me every step of this journey. Through Your divine power, I have everything I need. When doubt tries to return, remind me of the truth: I have what it takes because You are in me. Help me to walk in that confidence, encourage others with that hope, and live a life that reflects Your strength and grace. In Jesus' name, Amen.

Next Steps

Congratulations on completing the You Have What It Takes 30-day devotional! You have taken important steps to embrace your God-given purpose, discover your strength, and build your faith to live confidently and courageously.

Remember, this journey is just the beginning. The truths you have learned, the prayers you have prayed, and the reflections you've made are the foundation for a life lived by design — a life of intentional purpose, passion, and potential.

We all have a mountain to climb, and sometimes that mountain feels overwhelming and impossible to scale. But you don't have to climb it alone. If you are ready to take your growth even further, we invite you to join one of our transformational workshops at lifebydesign.net. These workshops offer deeper exploration, practical tools, and supportive community to help you move from discovery to action — turning your God-given dreams into reality.

Whether you want to clarify your purpose, develop leadership skills, or build habits for lasting change, Life by Design offers experiences designed to equip and empower you. You don't have to walk this journey alone.

Visit lifebydesign.net to find upcoming workshops, register, and connect with others who are on the same path of faith and growth.

Thank you for allowing us to walk alongside you through this devotional. Keep believing, keep stepping forward, and remember:

You truly have what it takes — because God is with you every step of the way.

May God bless you richly as you live your life by design.

References

Scripture References

All Scripture quotations are taken from:

- The Holy Bible, New International Version® (NIV)
- Copyright © 1973, 1978, 1984, 2011 by Biblica, Inc.™
- Used by permission. All rights reserved worldwide.

Other translations may be used throughout the devotional where noted:

- NKJV – New King James Version
- NLT – New Living Translation
- ESV – English Standard Version
- MSG – The Message Bible, Eugene H. Peterson

Inspirational Quotes

Includes quotes by Christine Caine, Brene Brown, Joyce Meyer, Charles Stanley, CS Lewis, Jane Goodall, Mark Black, Bethany Hamilton, Lao Tzu, Richard Wagner, Ambrose Redmoon, Dr. Robert H. Schuller and Unknown. Every effort has been made to give credit to the original sources. If any quotes are found to be incorrectly attributed, please contact us at info@lifebydesign.net for correction in future editions.

Acknowledgments

To everyone who has ever felt unqualified or not enough — this is for you.

To Jesus Christ — the One who calls, equips, and strengthens. All glory to Him.

To our family, mentors, and the Life by Design leadership team to include Dan Williams, Danny and Christie Duarte, Kevin Suess and Jill Conway— thank you for believing in this message and the ministry of Life by Design.

We would like to thank the following individuals for encouraging us on our life journey, Dan Williams, Jill Conway, Ken and Anita Van Wyk, Ron Glosser, Fred Smith Sr, Brenda Smith, Dr. Robert H. Schuller, Harold Shaw, Jane Emberty, Jim Coleman and Norm Hatfield.

About Life by Design

Life by Design is a nonprofit organization dedicated to helping individuals discover and live out their God-given purpose. Through coaching, workshops, and resources, they aim to inspire people to live and lead like Jesus, fostering personal, professional, and spiritual growth.

Mission and Vision

- **Mission**: To encourage and equip others to know God and make Him known by helping them discover their God-given purpose and mission, inspiring them to be the person God created them to be, and leaving a legacy of faith.

- **Vision**: To provide coaching, training, and resources to individuals and groups to encourage, equip, and inspire them to be the person God intended them to be.

Workshops and Programs

Life by Design offers a variety of workshops and programs designed to help individuals align their lives with their purpose.

Online Resources

In addition to in-person workshops, Life by Design offers free online courses, podcasts, and video series featuring special guest speakers. These resources aim to inspire, transform, and equip individuals to be all they are called to be.

Testimonials

Participants have shared positive feedback about their experiences:

"Life by Design is a course that brings an immense amount of personal insight to an individual who wants to seek more purpose and Godly inspiration to their life." - **Debbie Lips**

"I would definitely recommend Life by Design to others. Many times people do not take the time to get off the wheel of life to just to think and ask themselves lives important questions. Participating in Life by Design causes you to stop and think and ask the important questions and listen to what the spirit of God is saying to you."
- **Harold Shaw**

"The Life By Design program stood out as each session built a pathway for examination of self-understanding – opening the opportunity for each individual to turn their potentials into significant growth steps." **-Norm Hatfield**

"Life by Design is a tool that can help re-focus your present and equip you to spend the rest of your life living on purpose! But like any tool in the tool box, you have to use it. And when you do, you will be better for it. I strongly urge you to consider living your Life by Design" **-Kevin Suess**

For more information on Life by Design or to register for upcoming workshops, visit LifeByDesign.Net or write to us at findyourpurpose@lifebydesign.net

About Bob and Michelle Cavinder

Bob Cavinder is an accomplished trainer, facilitator, and leadership coach with over two decades of experience designing and delivering transformative learning experiences across the hospitality and nonprofit sectors including the Crystal Cathedral Ministries. As Executive Director and Director of Training and Development for Life by Design, Bob equips leaders and frontline teams through dynamic, strengths-based coaching, interactive workshops, and customized training solutions rooted in personal growth, customer service excellence, and transformational leadership. A certified trainer with the John Maxwell Team, Franklin Covey, Lead Like Jesus and Ziglar training, Bob combines practical leadership insight with engaging facilitation to inspire performance and purpose. His ability to develop leadership pipelines, strengthen team culture, and align training with organizational strategy makes him a trusted partner for both executive leaders and emerging talent alike.

Michelle Cavinder is a dynamic trainer, facilitator, and leadership coach with over two decades of experience empowering individuals and teams to grow, connect, and perform at their best. Drawing from a diverse background at the Crystal Cathedral in ministry, nonprofit leadership, and executive administration, Michelle is known for her ability to engage, inspire, and bring clarity to complex organizational and personal development challenges. As a Certified Facilitator in **The 7 Habits of Highly Effective Families** and a Certified Leadership Coach, she leverages her Gallup Strengths—Maximizer, Activator, Woo, Communication, and Focus—to create transformative training environments that build on natural strengths and unlock potential. Whether coaching senior leaders, leading team development sessions, or facilitating growth experiences, Michelle brings warmth, wisdom, and a proven ability to turn vision into action.